STANDING ON GUARD FOR THEE.

A Photography Zine Shot On Film By: Jason Kilroe

This zine is dedicated to all of you who unapologetically demonstrated what it means to be Canadian in 2020 and 2021. I hope that you will enjoy these photographs as much as I enjoyed taking them. Let this zine serve as a reminder to anyone who has felt alone during the past two years that the 'small fringe minority' was never really that small at all...

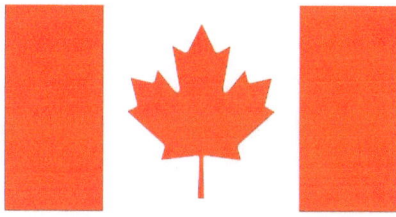

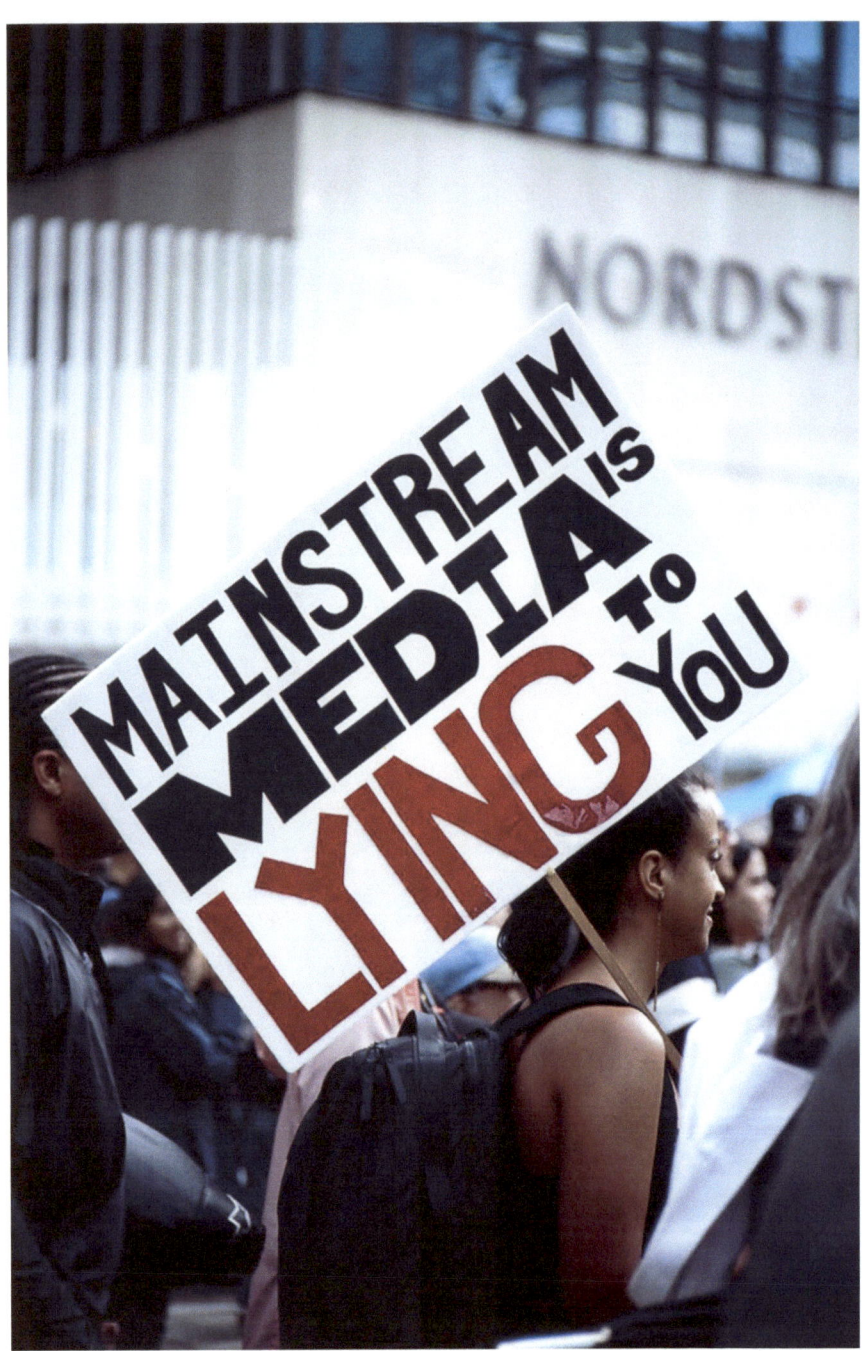

Kodak Ektachrome E100

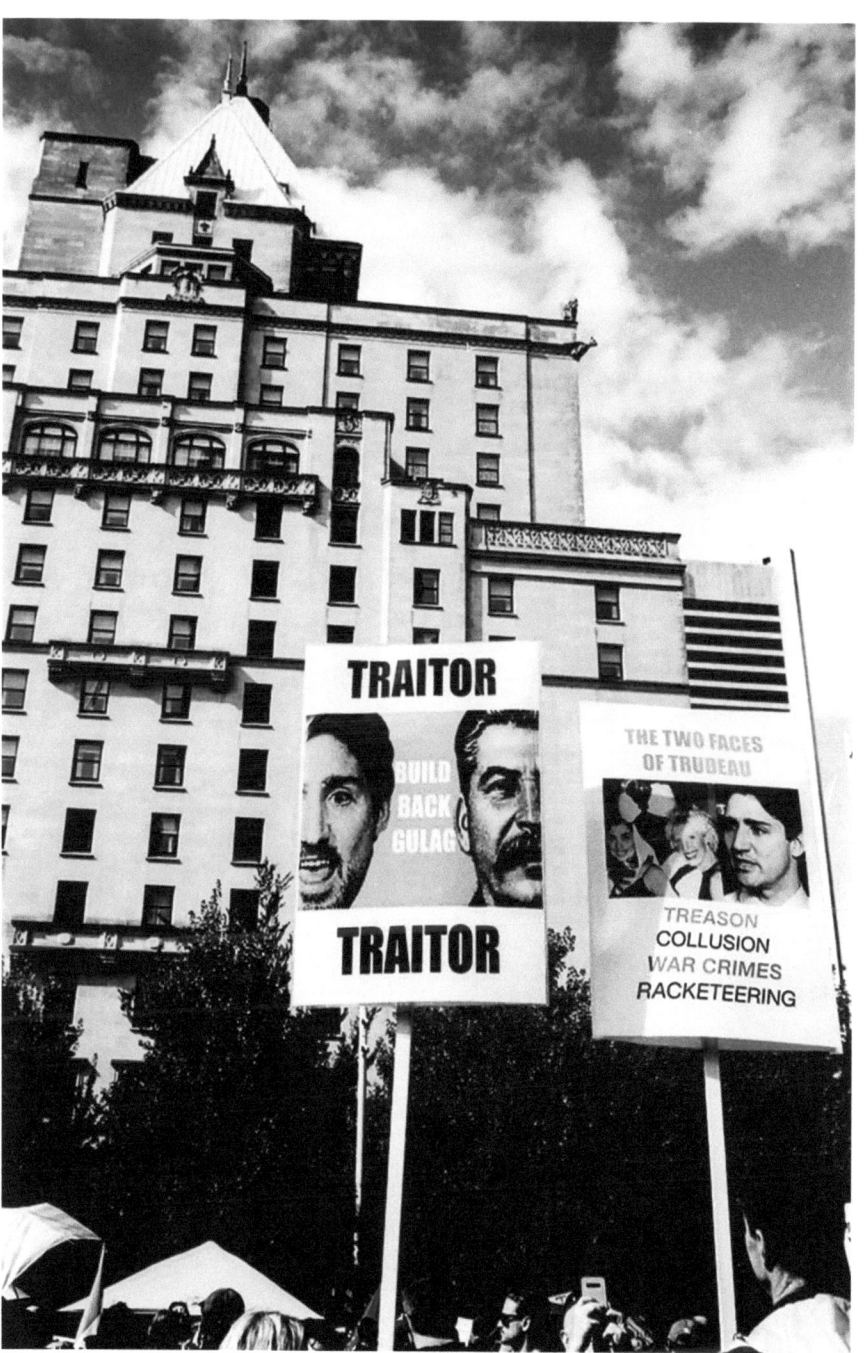

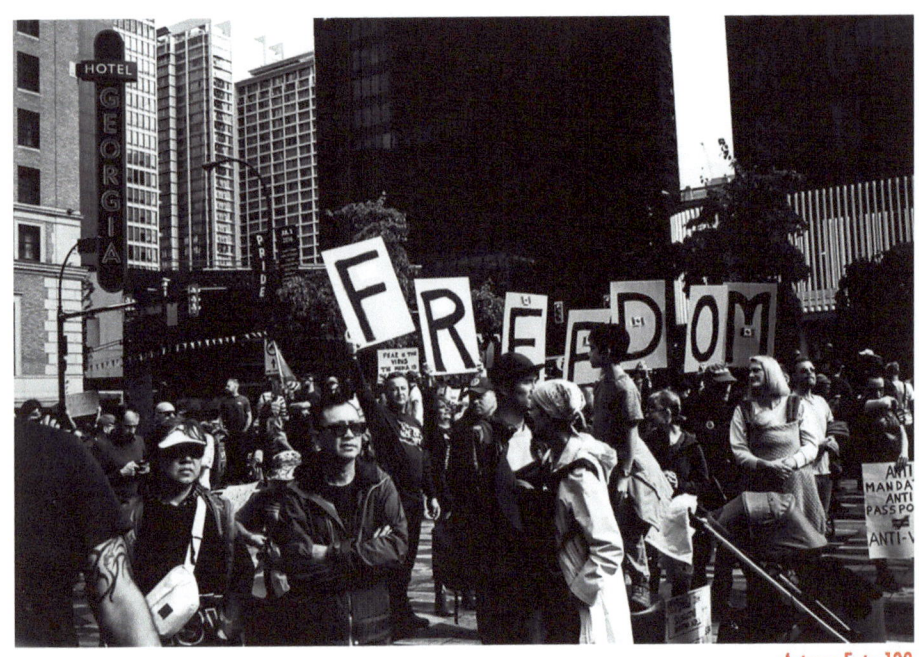

Astrum Foto 100

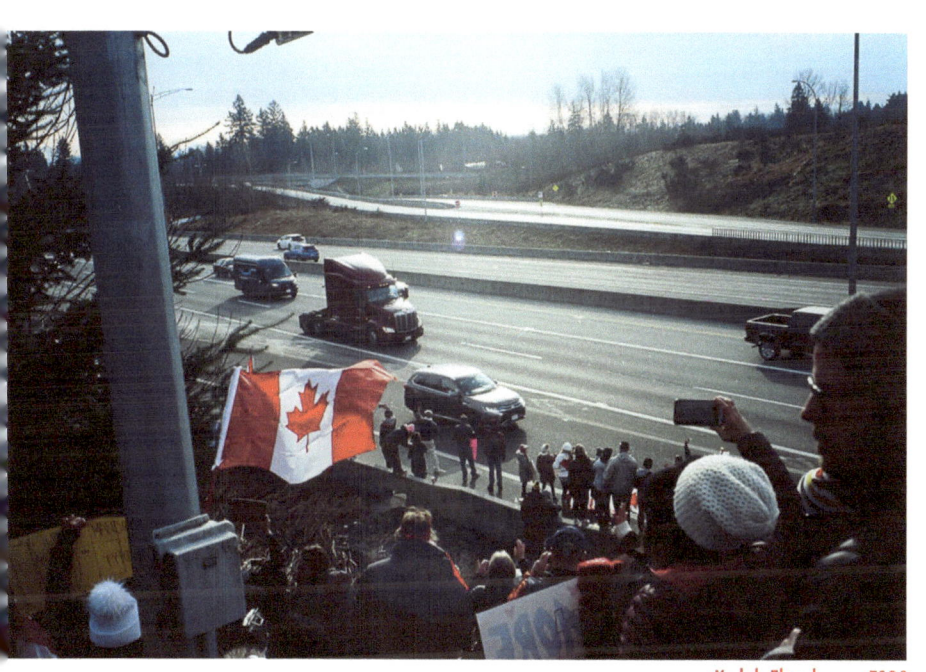

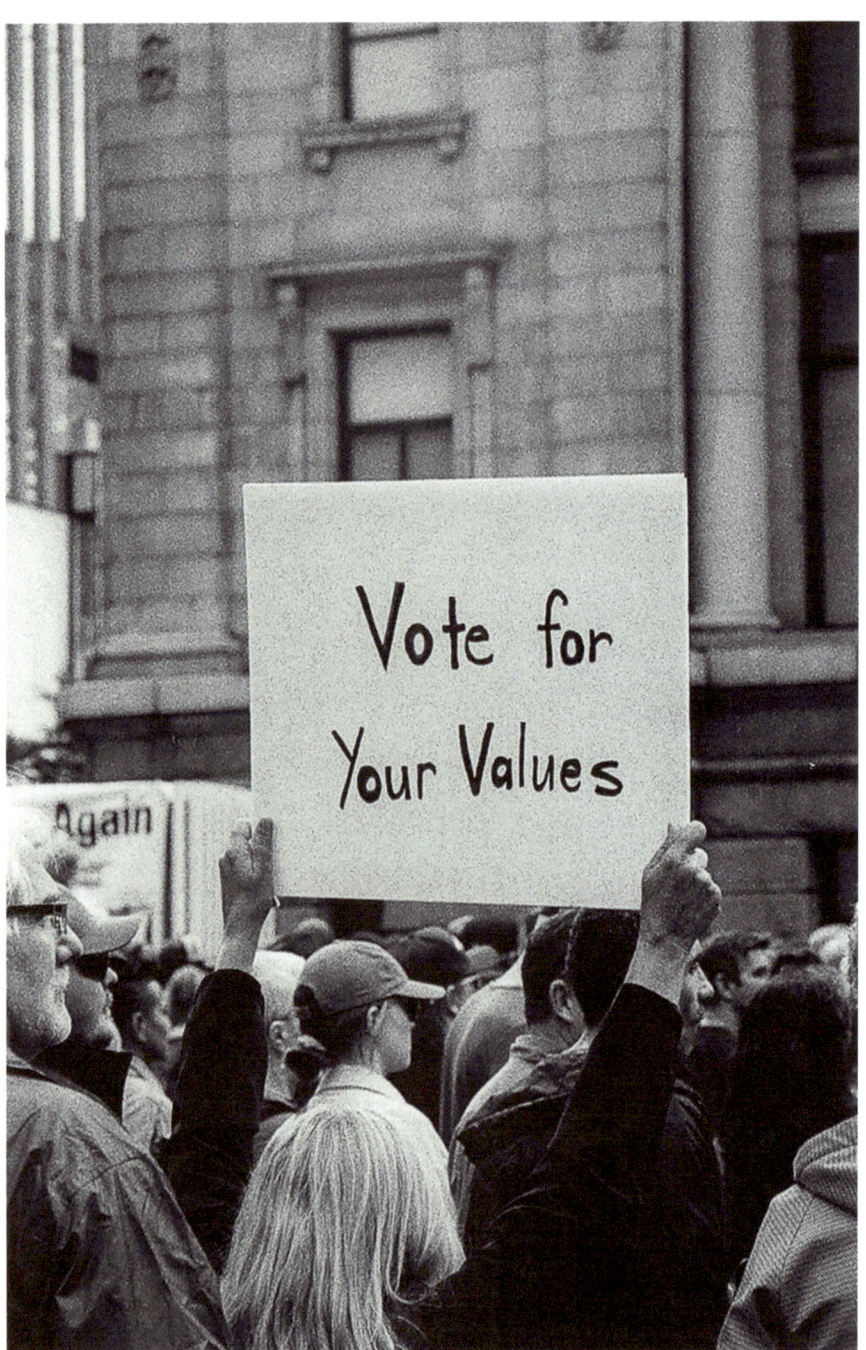

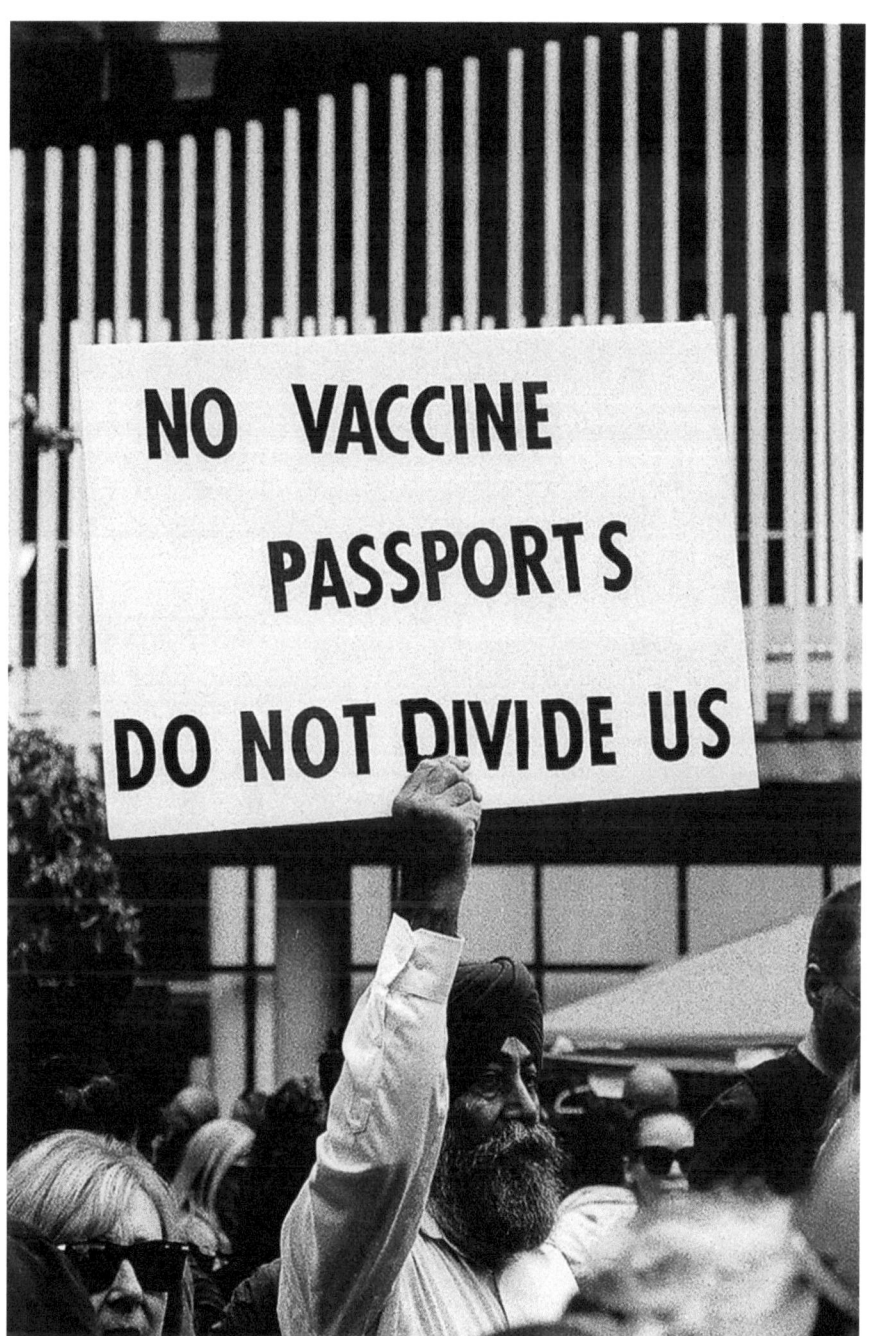

Ilford HP5 Plus

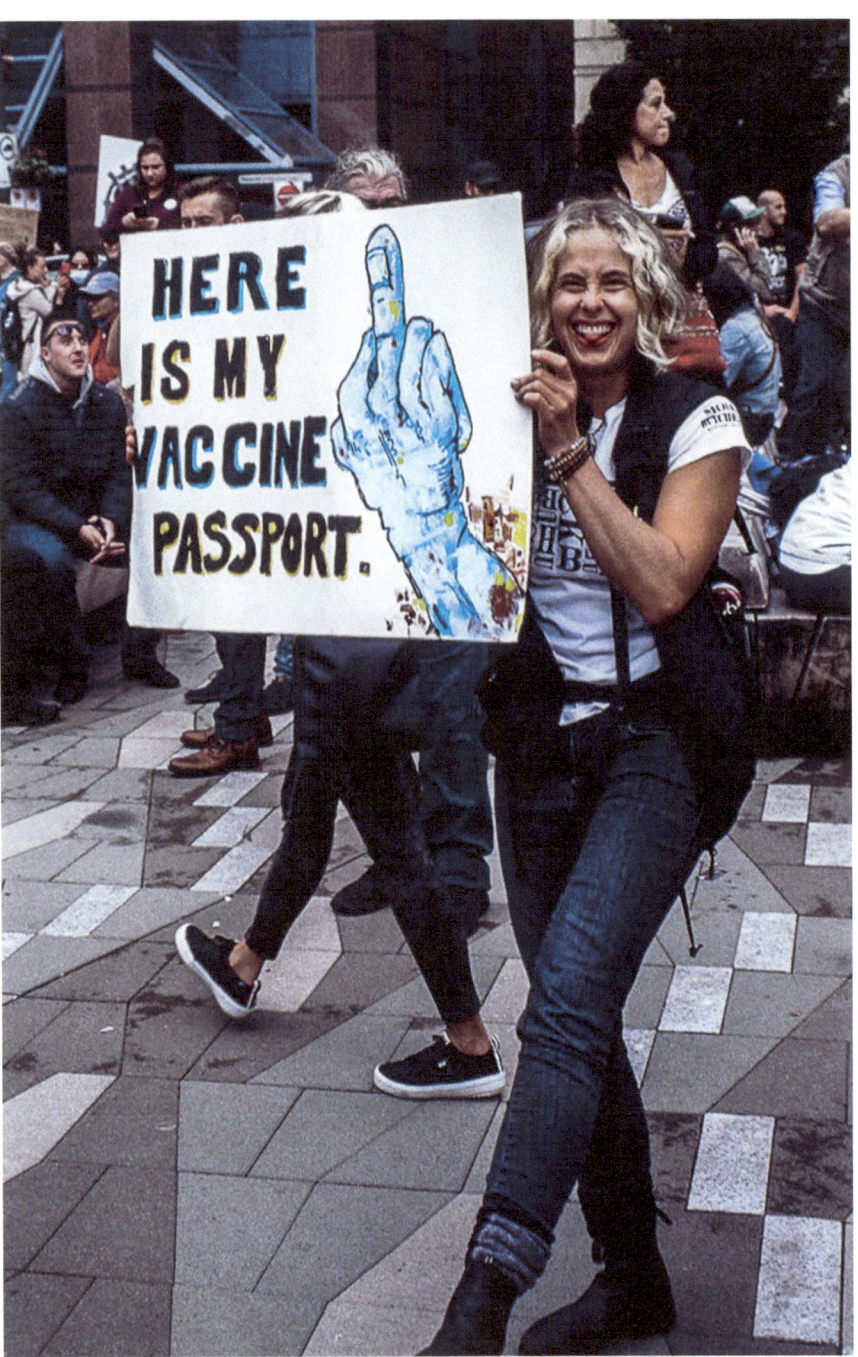

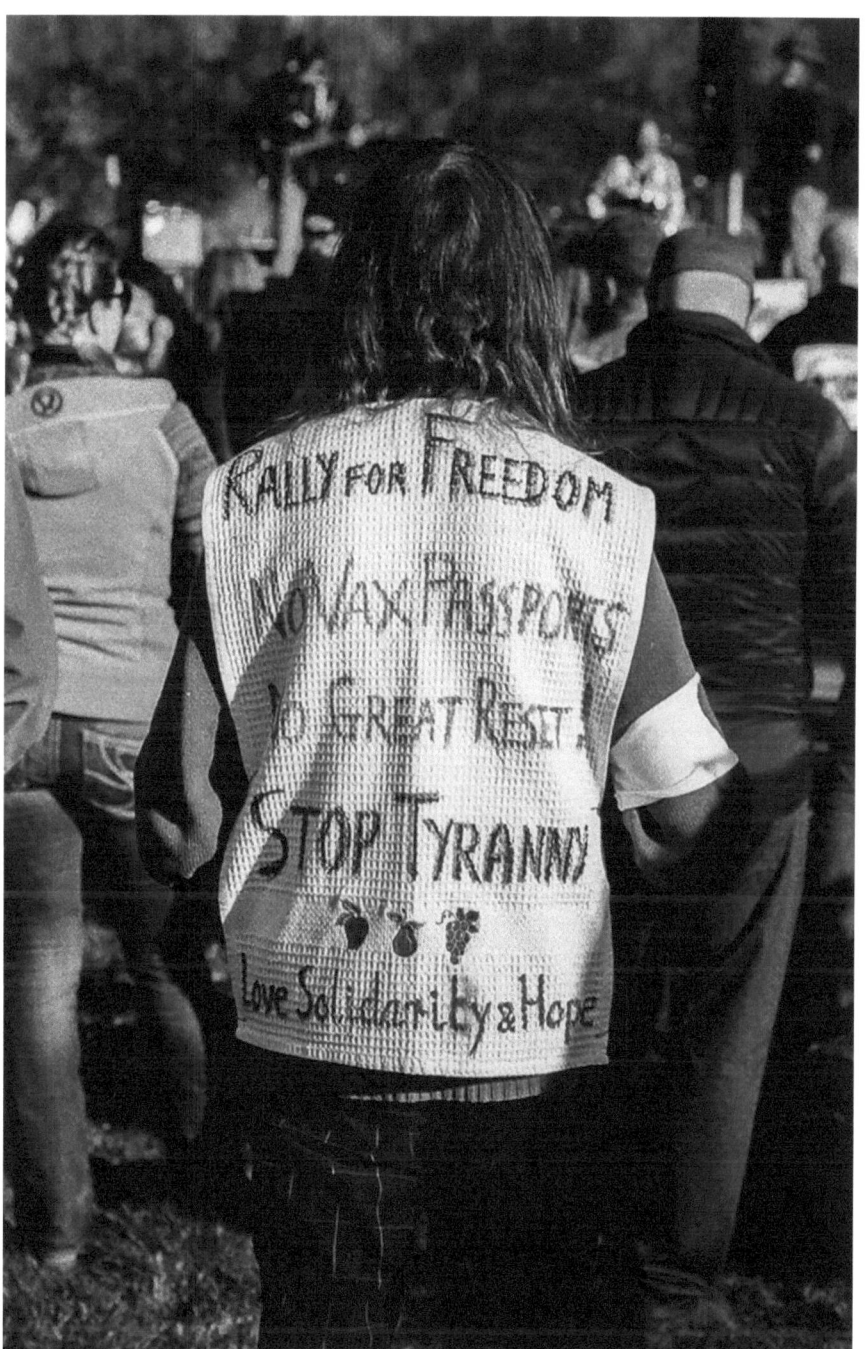

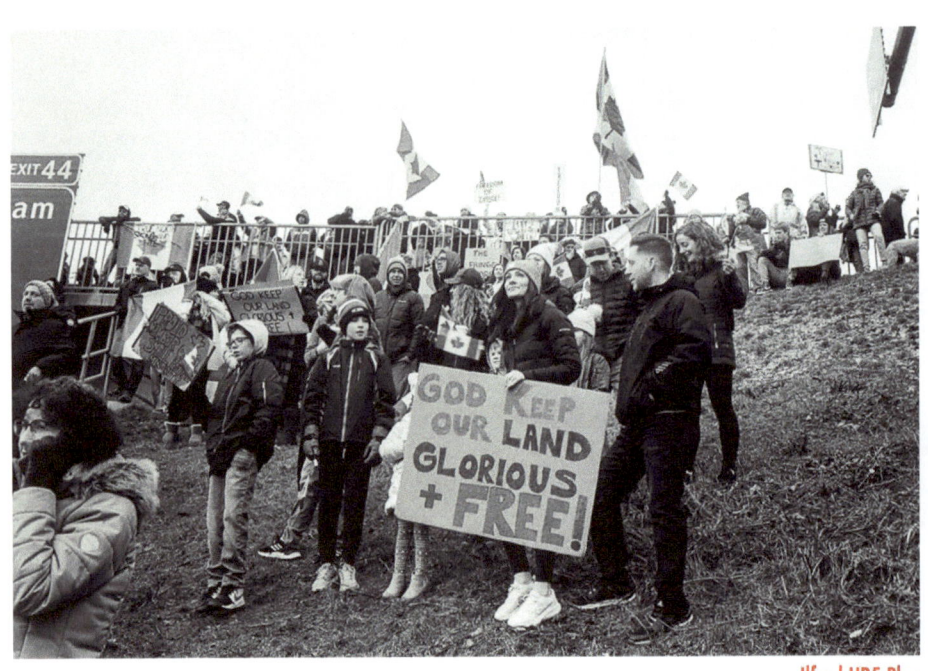

Ilford HP5 Plus

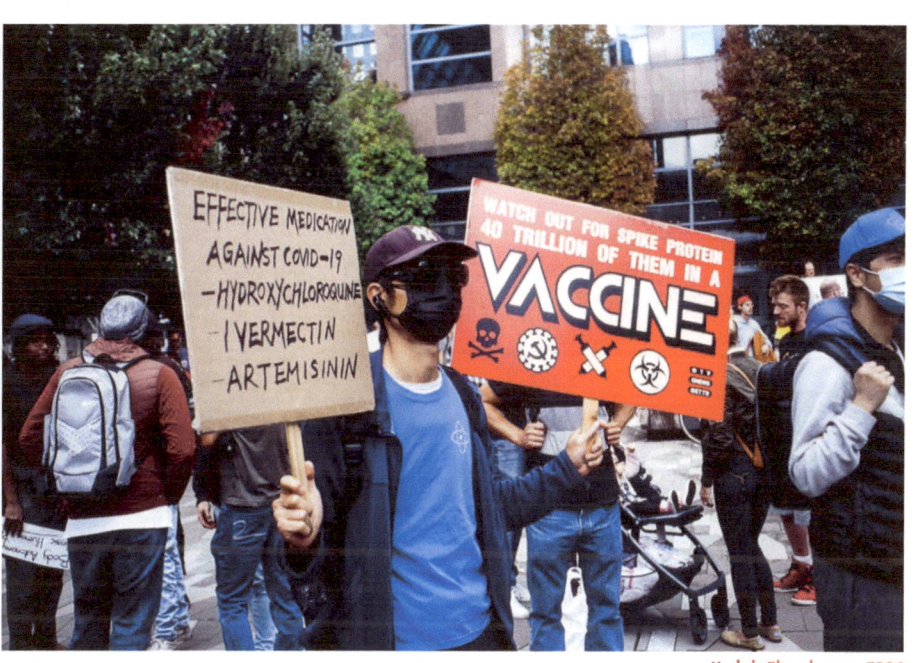

Kodak Ektachrome E100

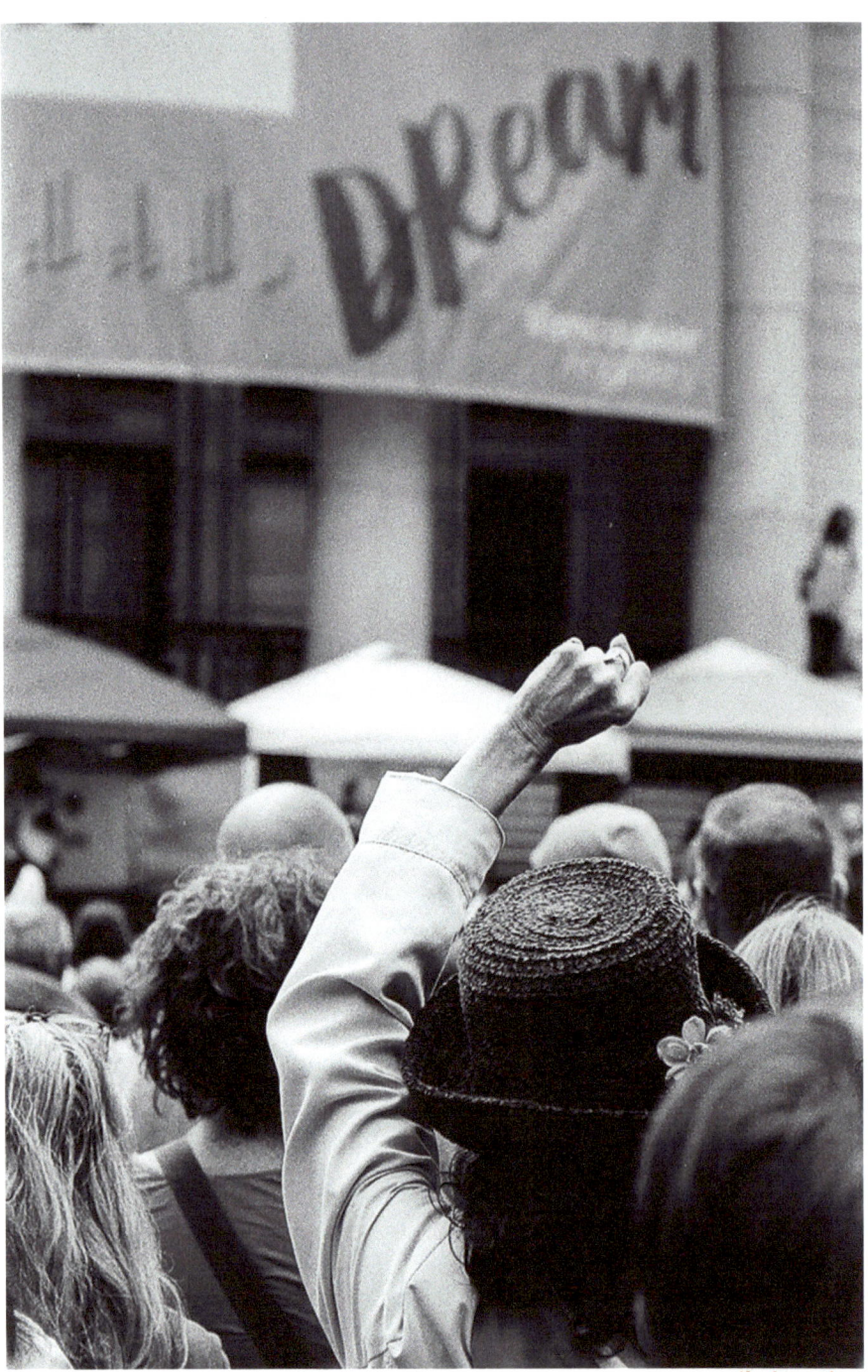

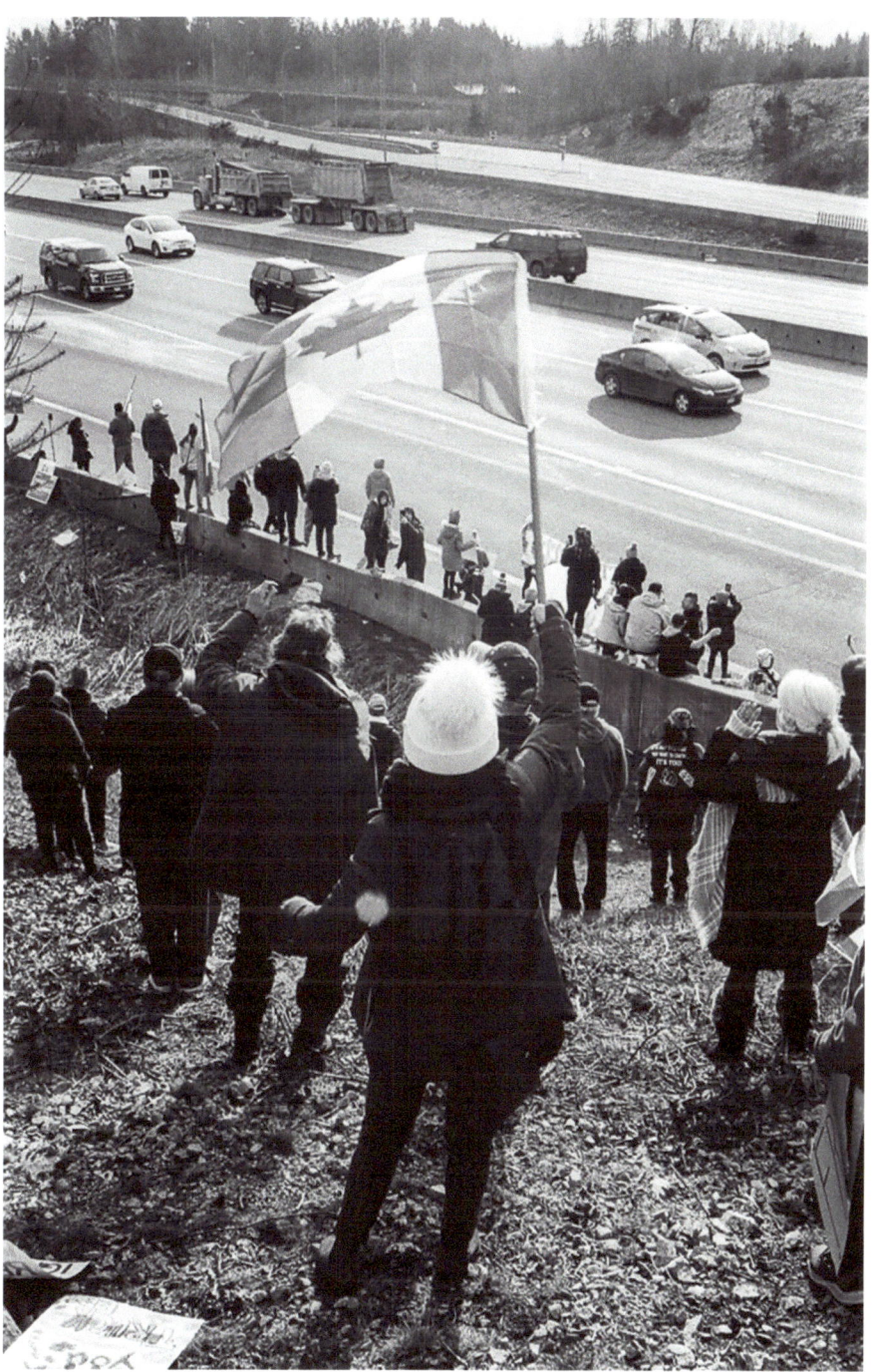

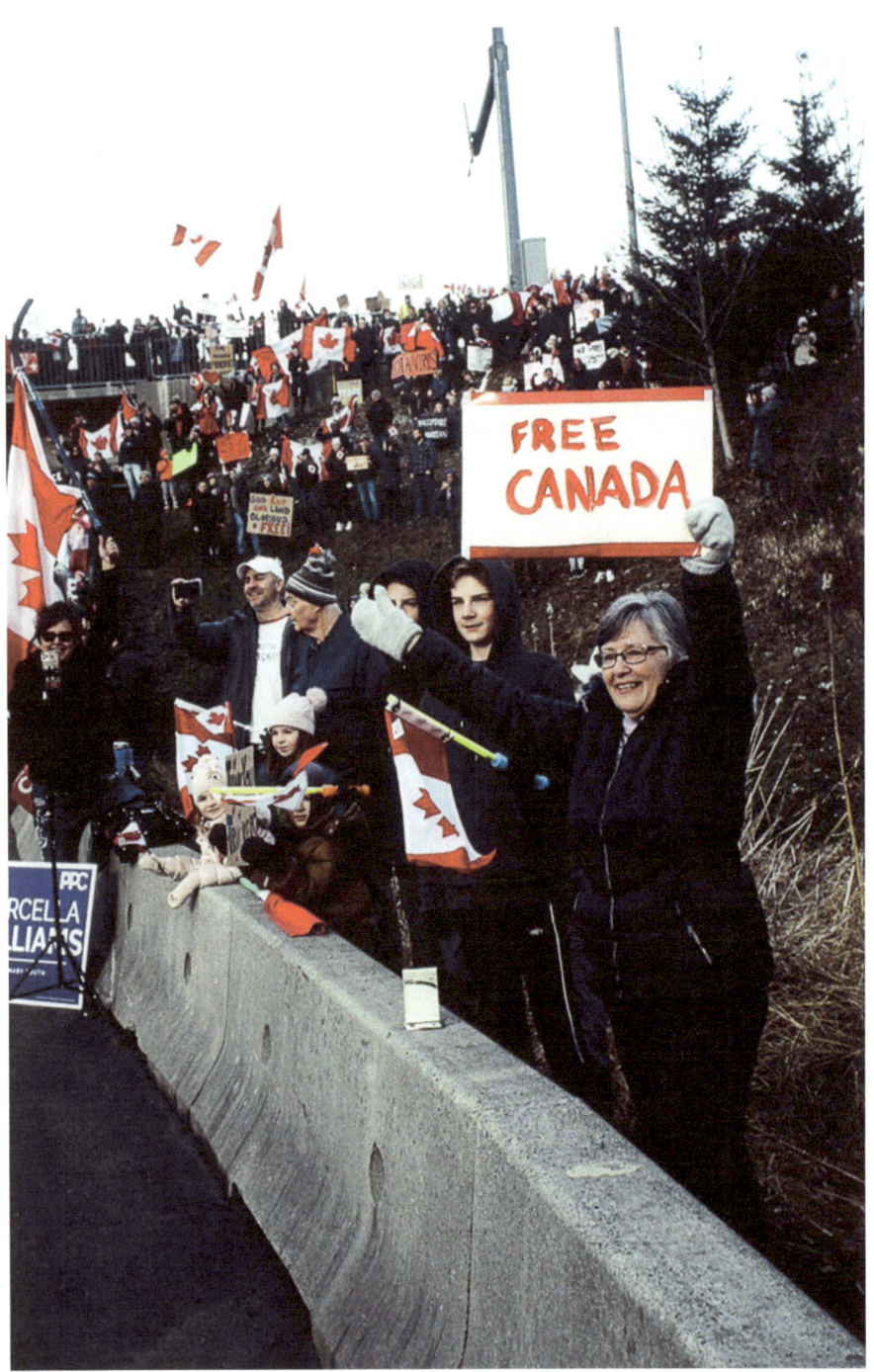

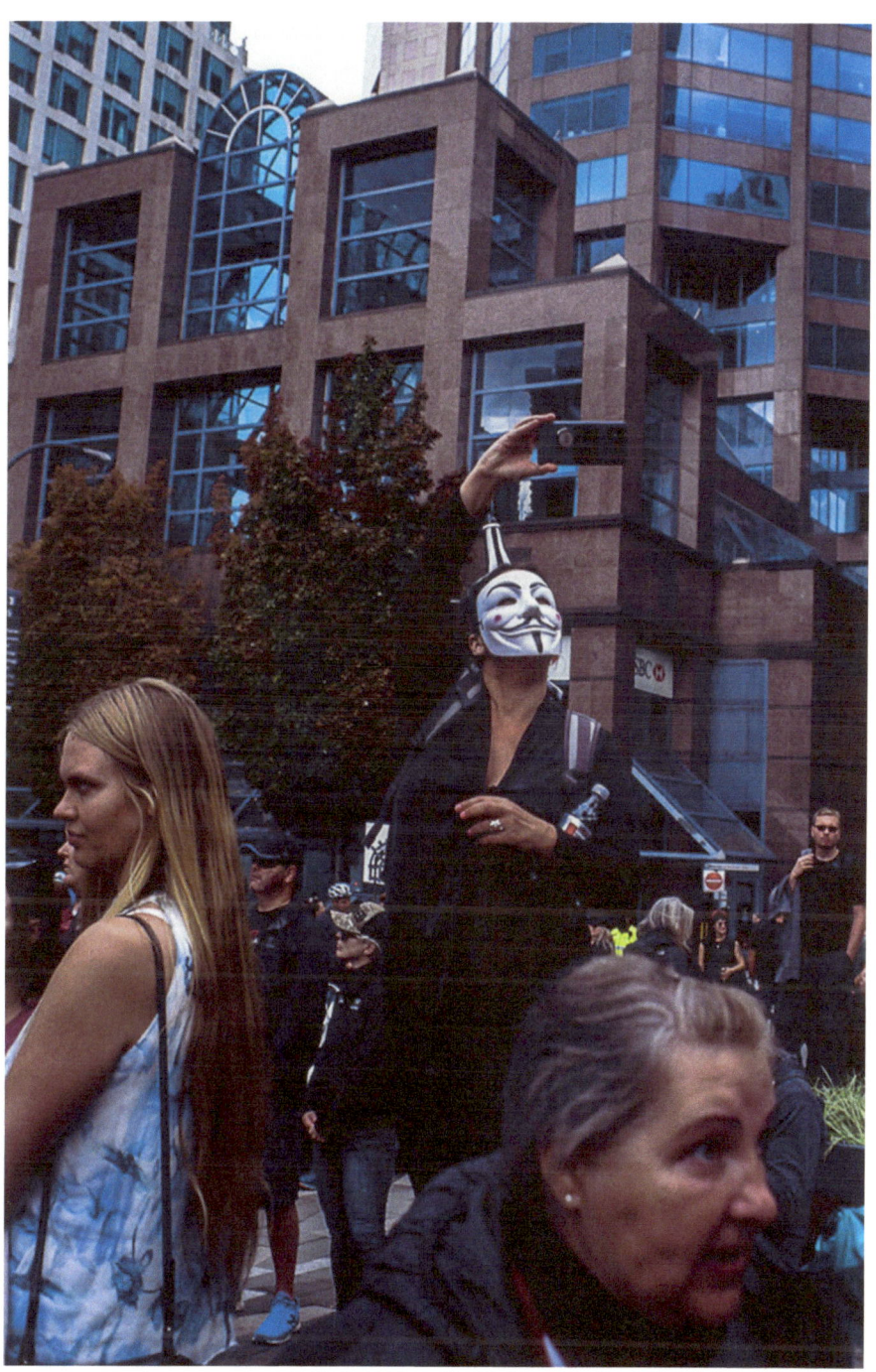

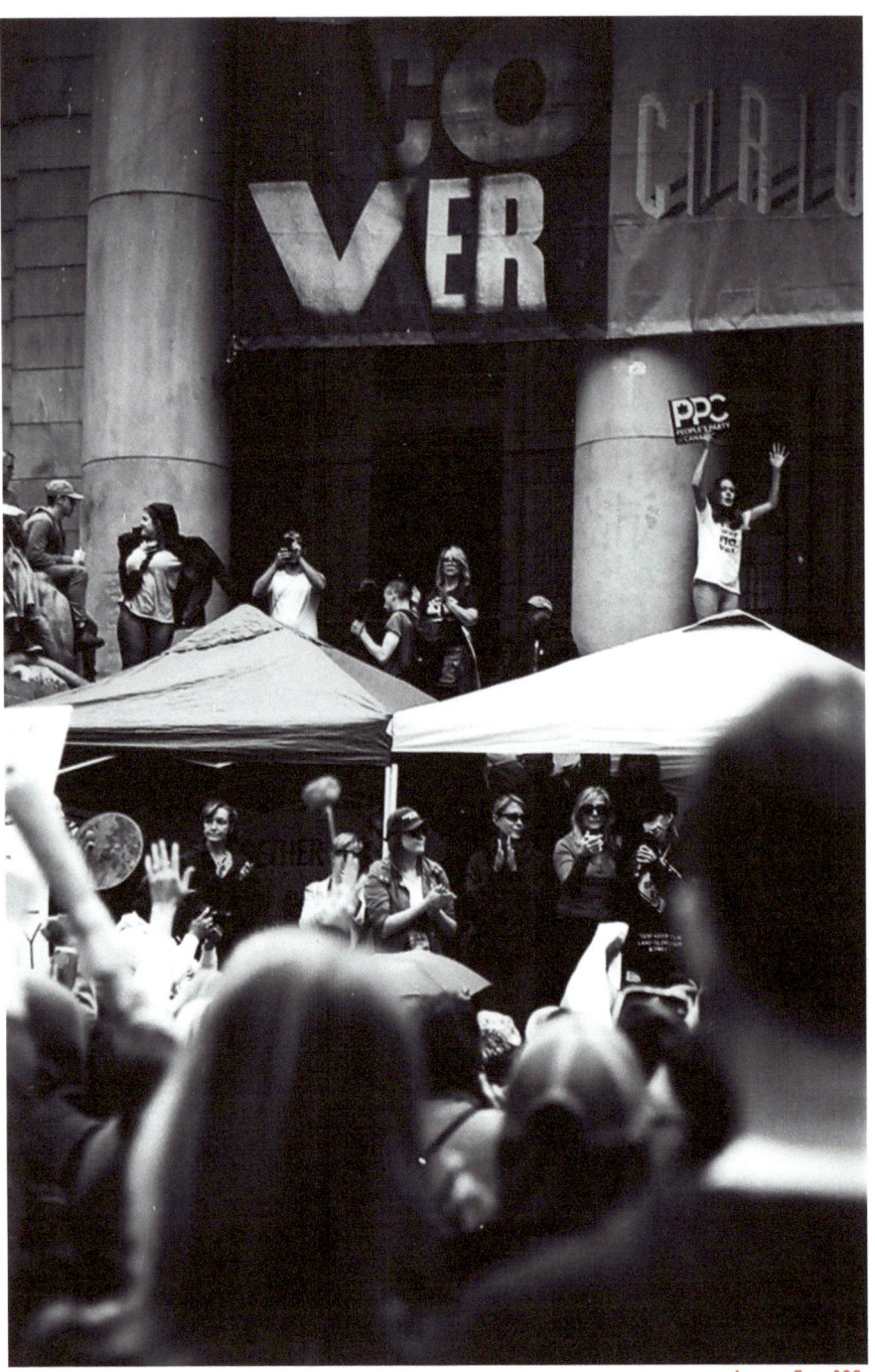

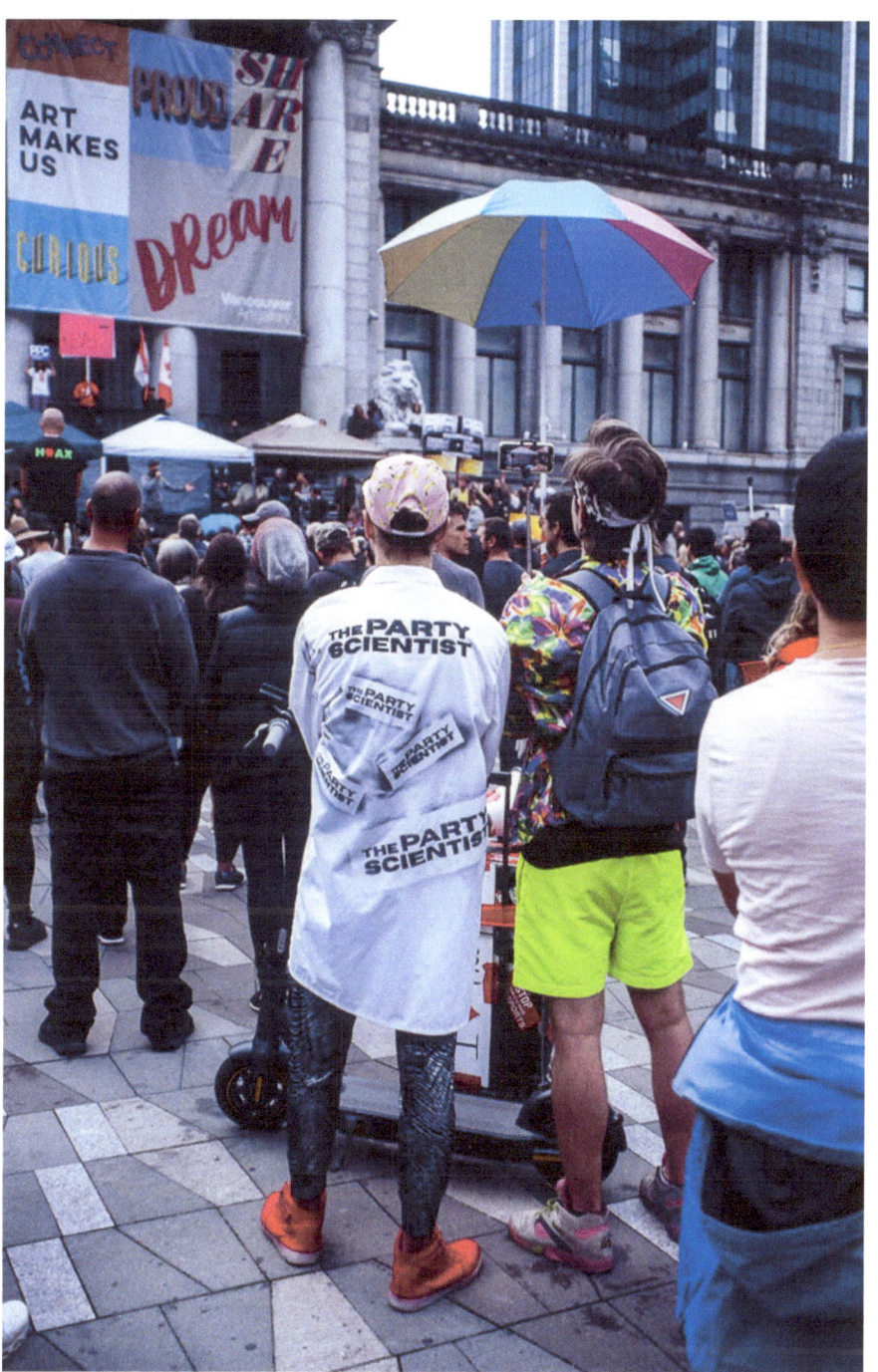

Kodak Ektachrome E100

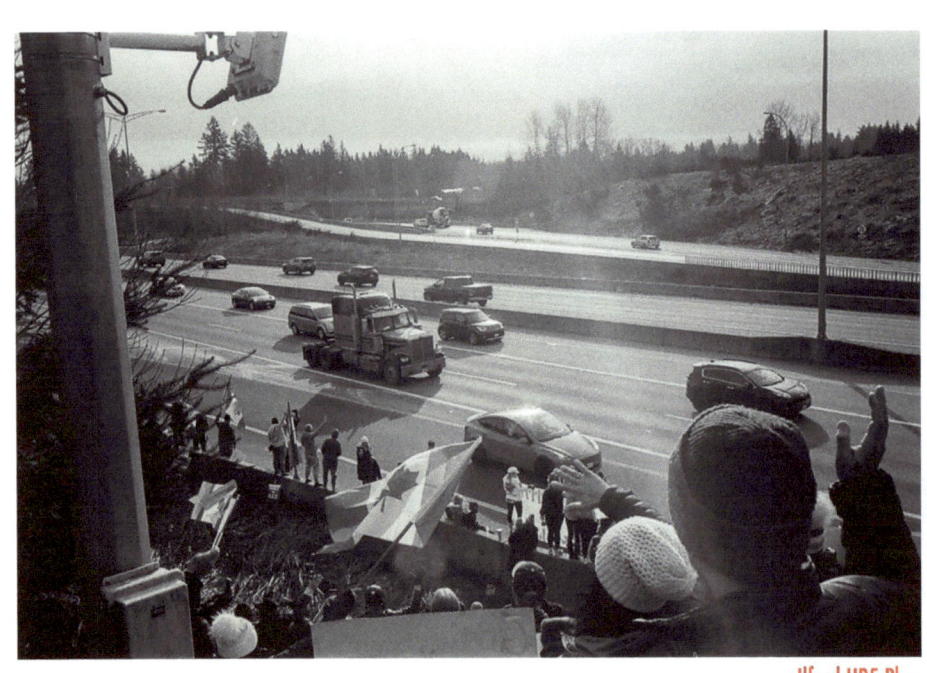

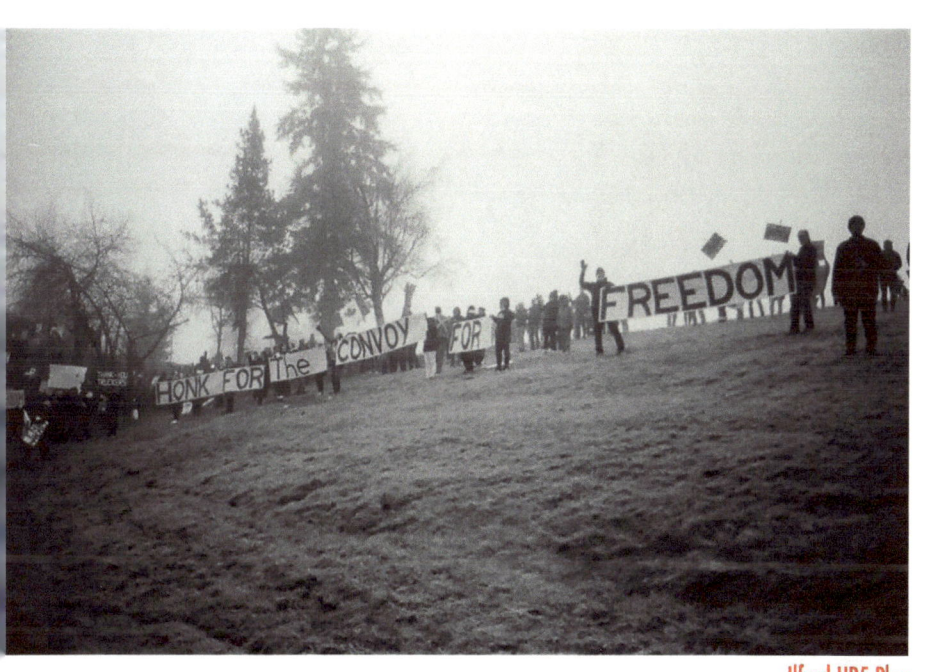

Ilford HP5 Plus

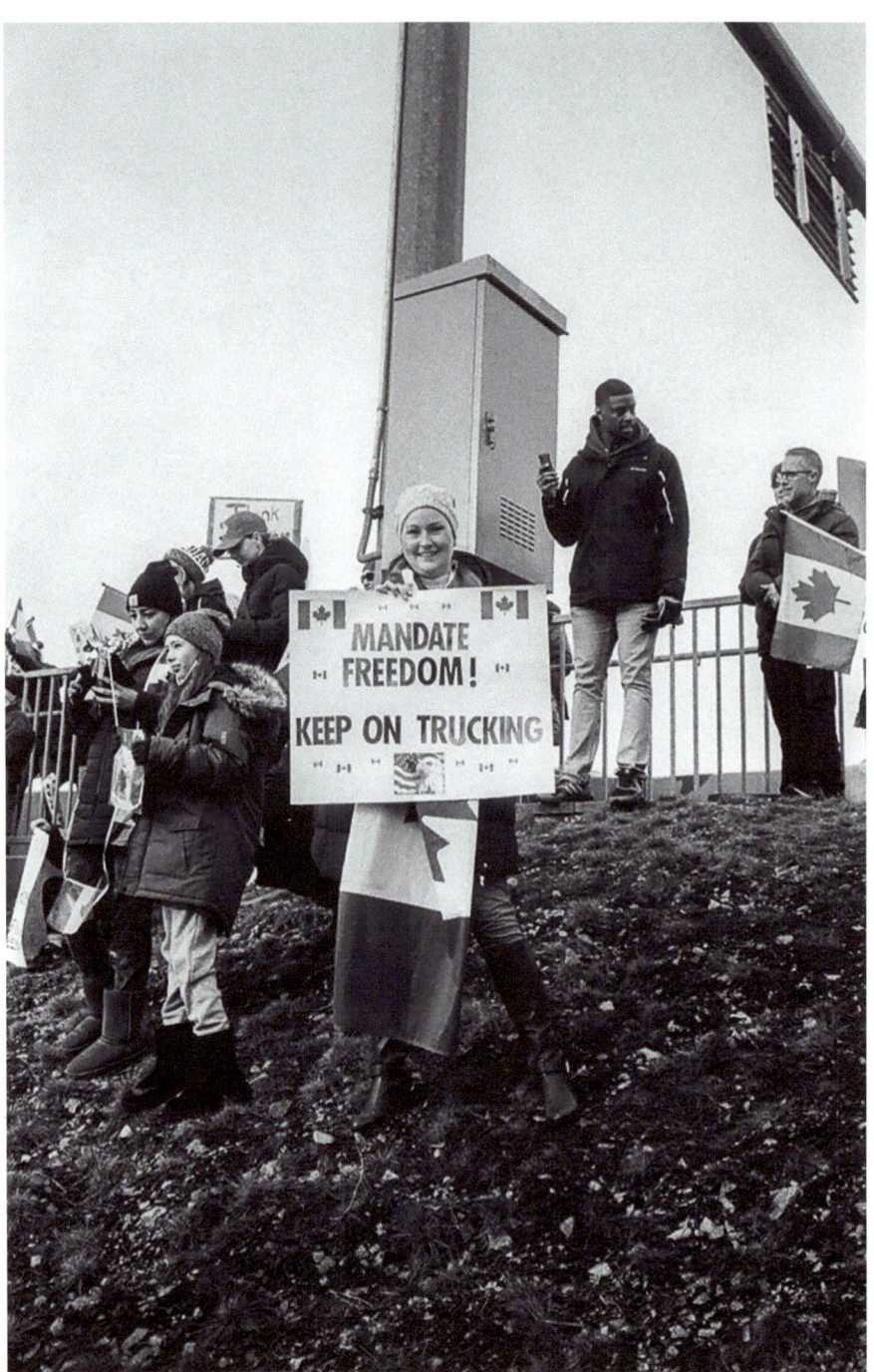

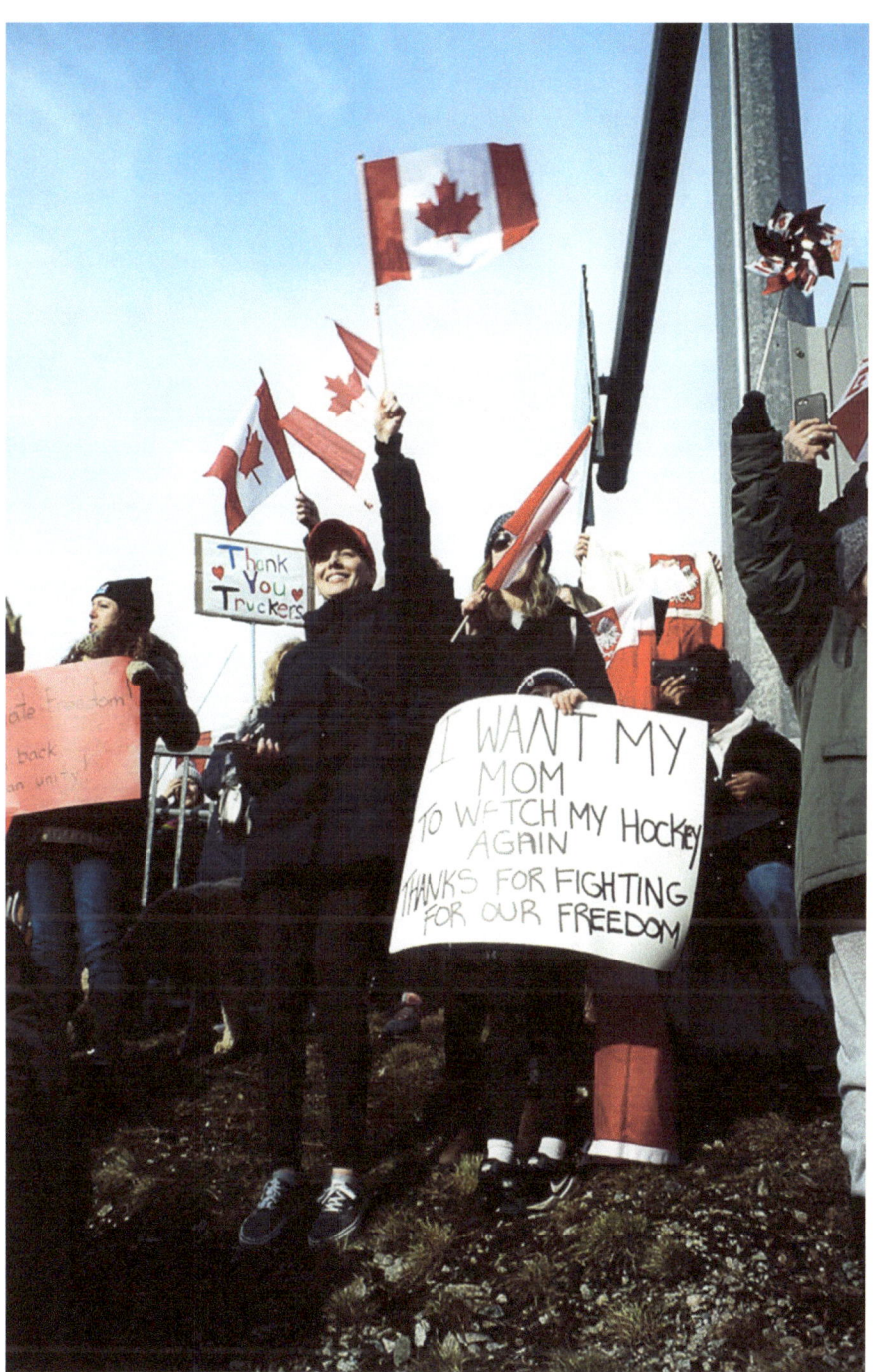

Kodak Ektachrome E100

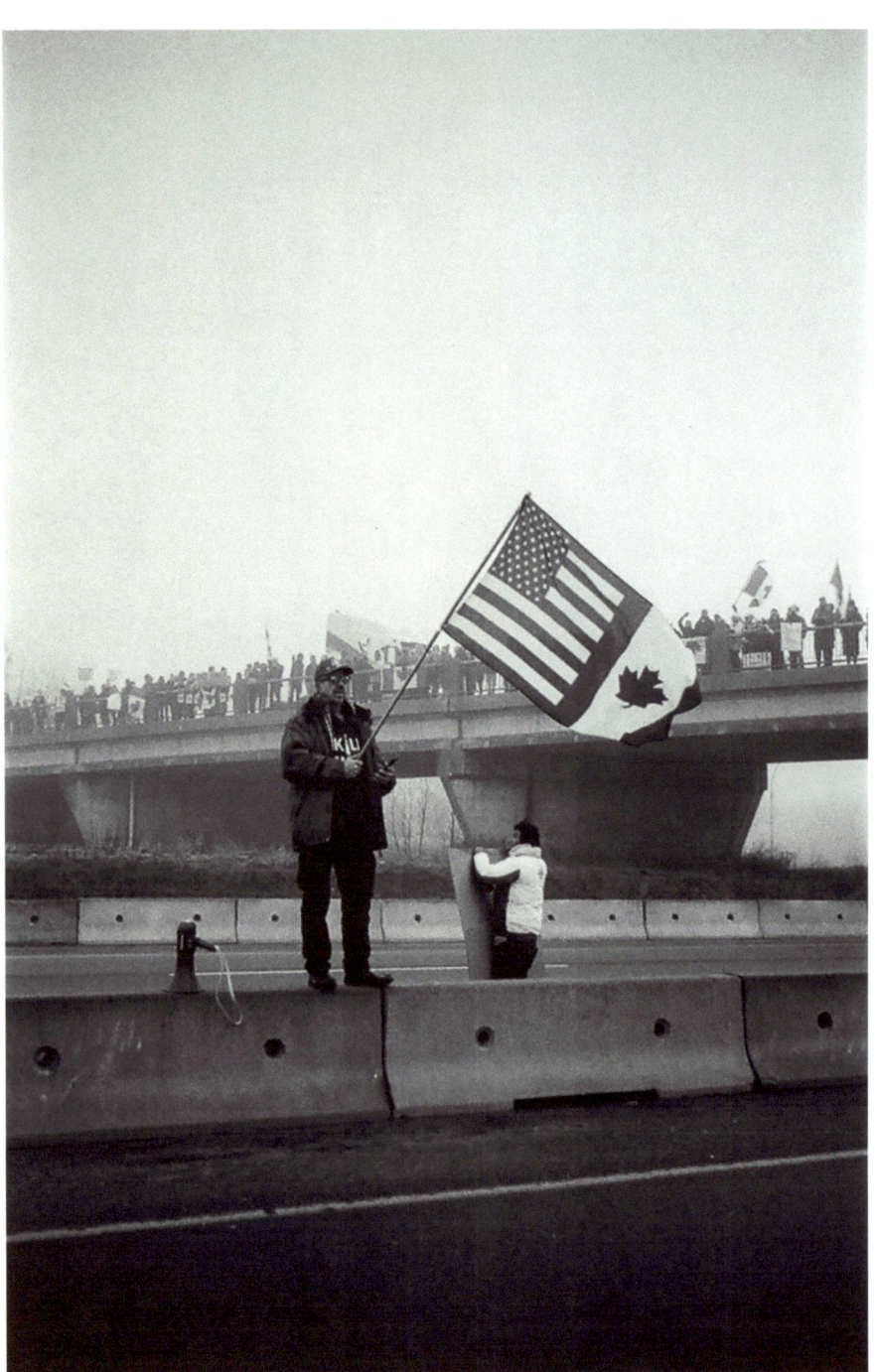

Ilford HP5 Plus

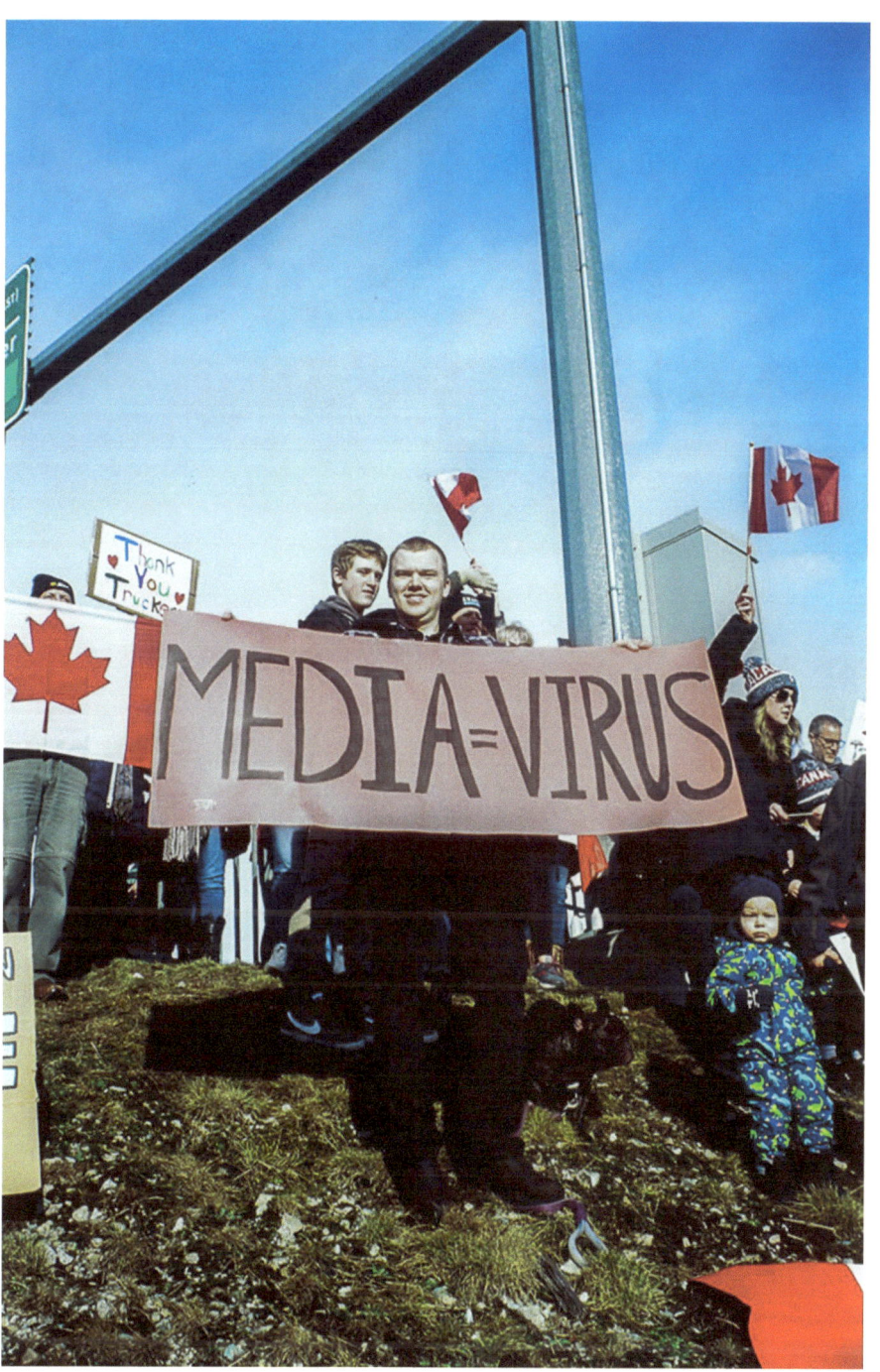

Kodak Ektachrome E100

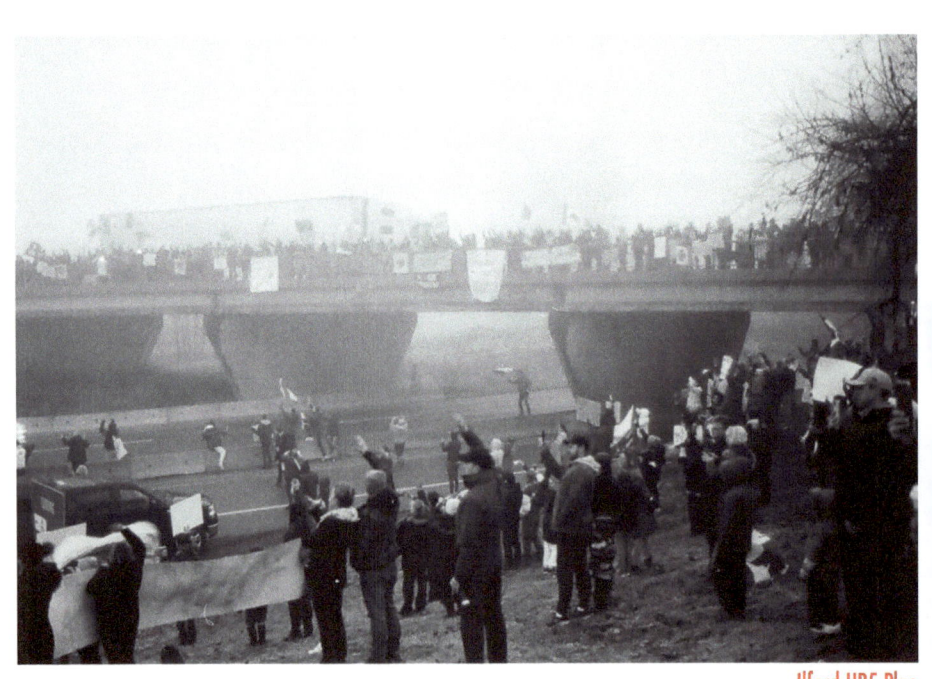

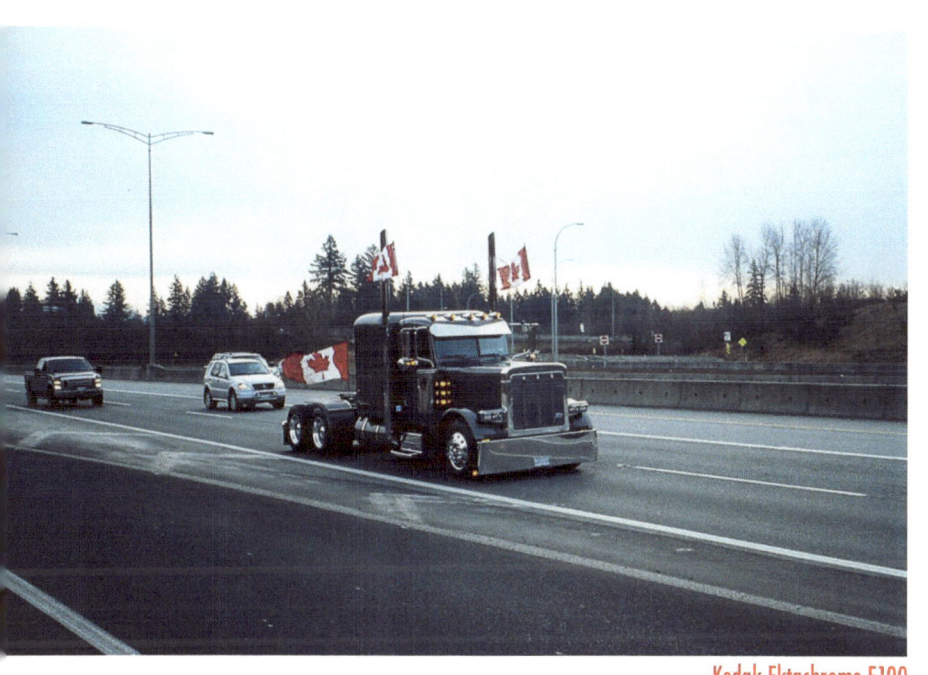

Kodak Ektachrome E100

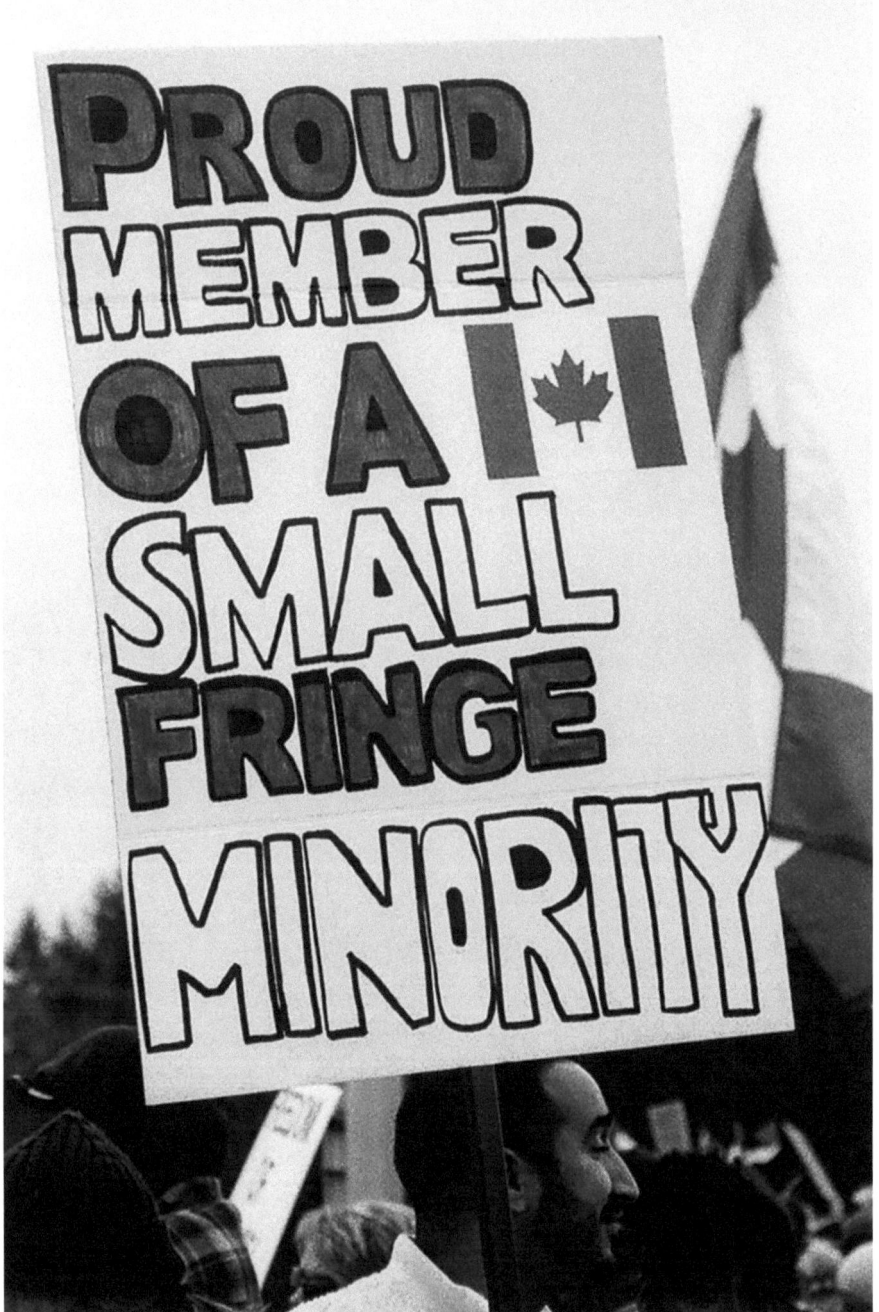

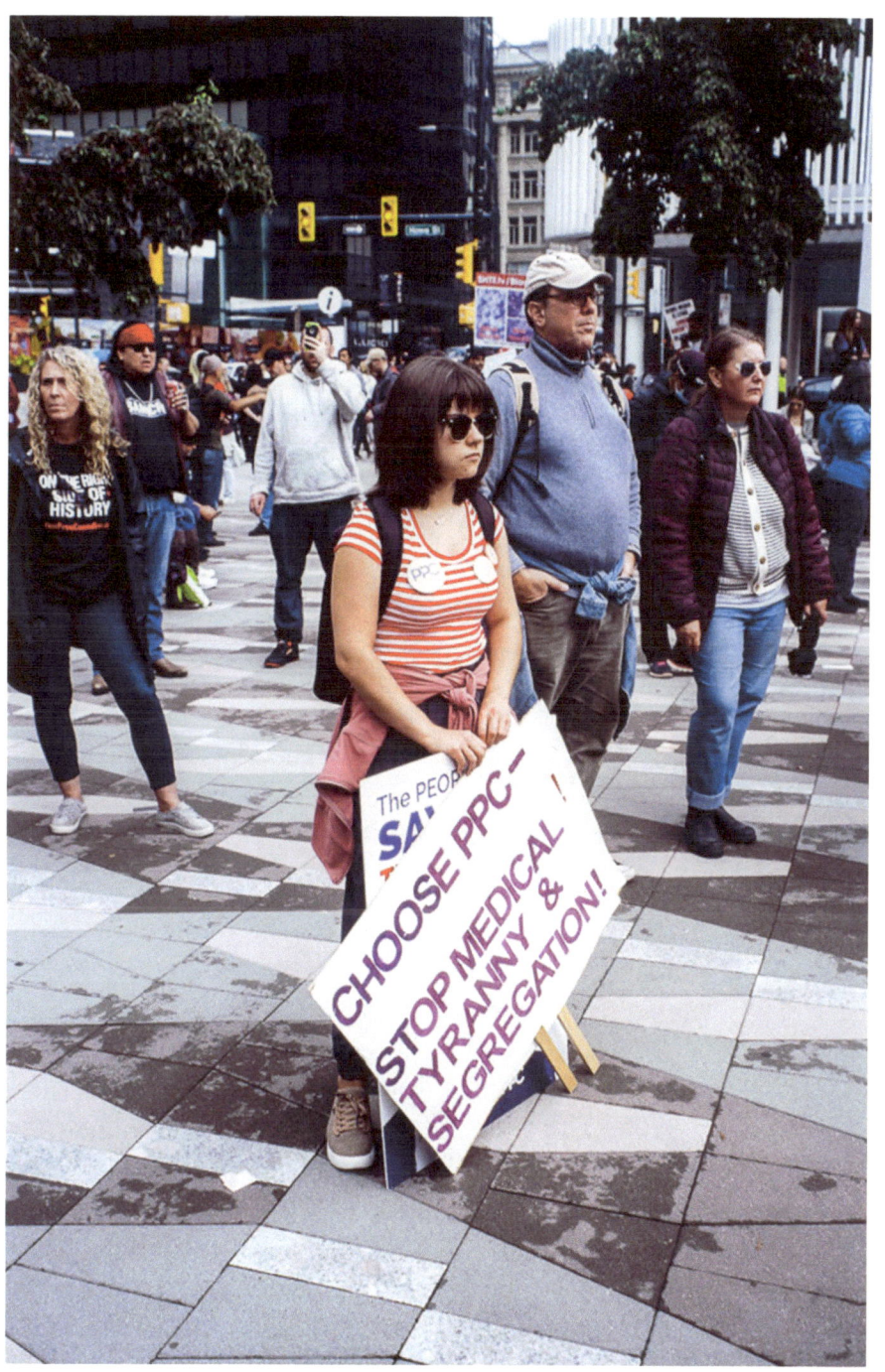

Kodak Ektachrome E100

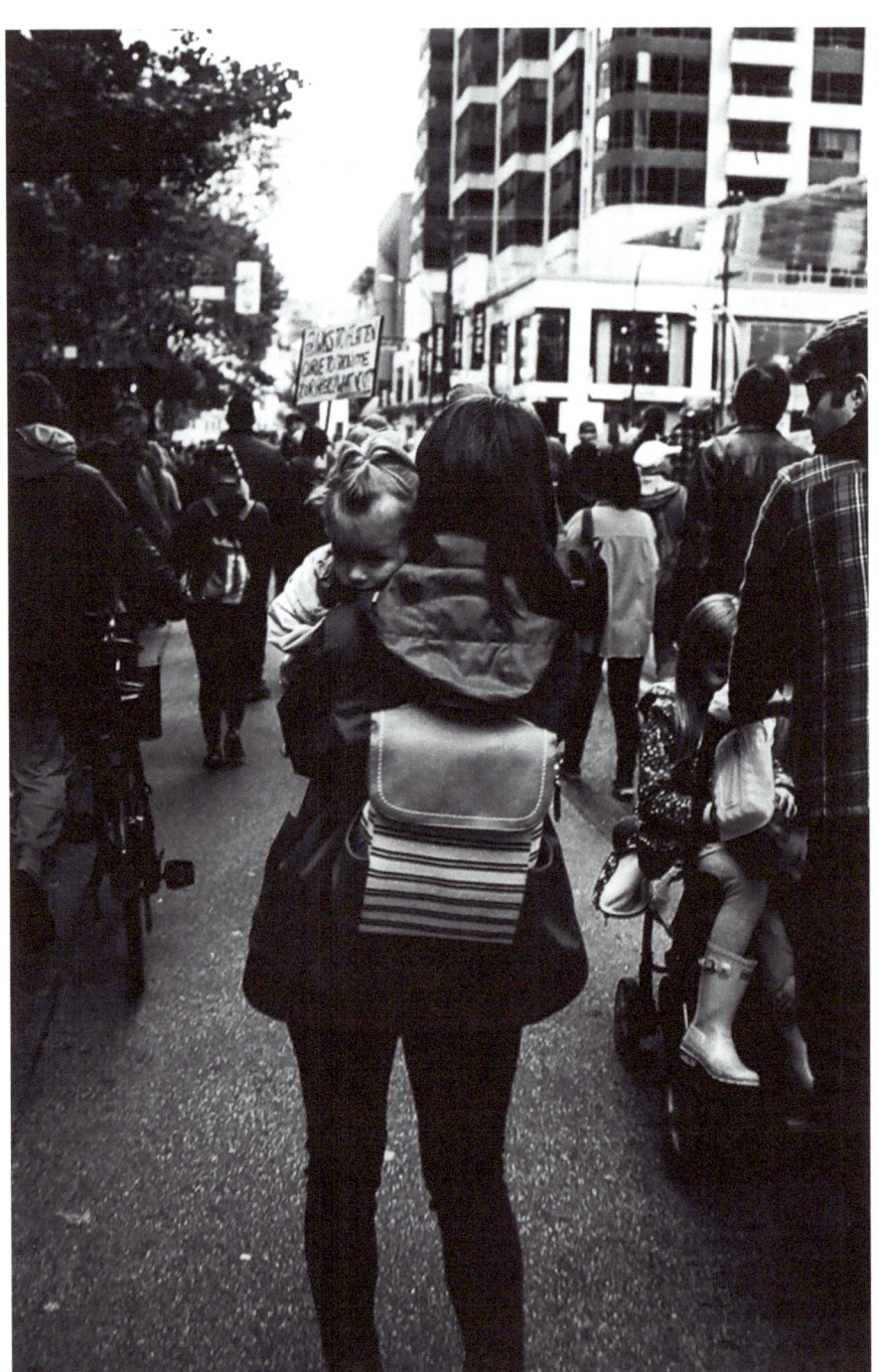

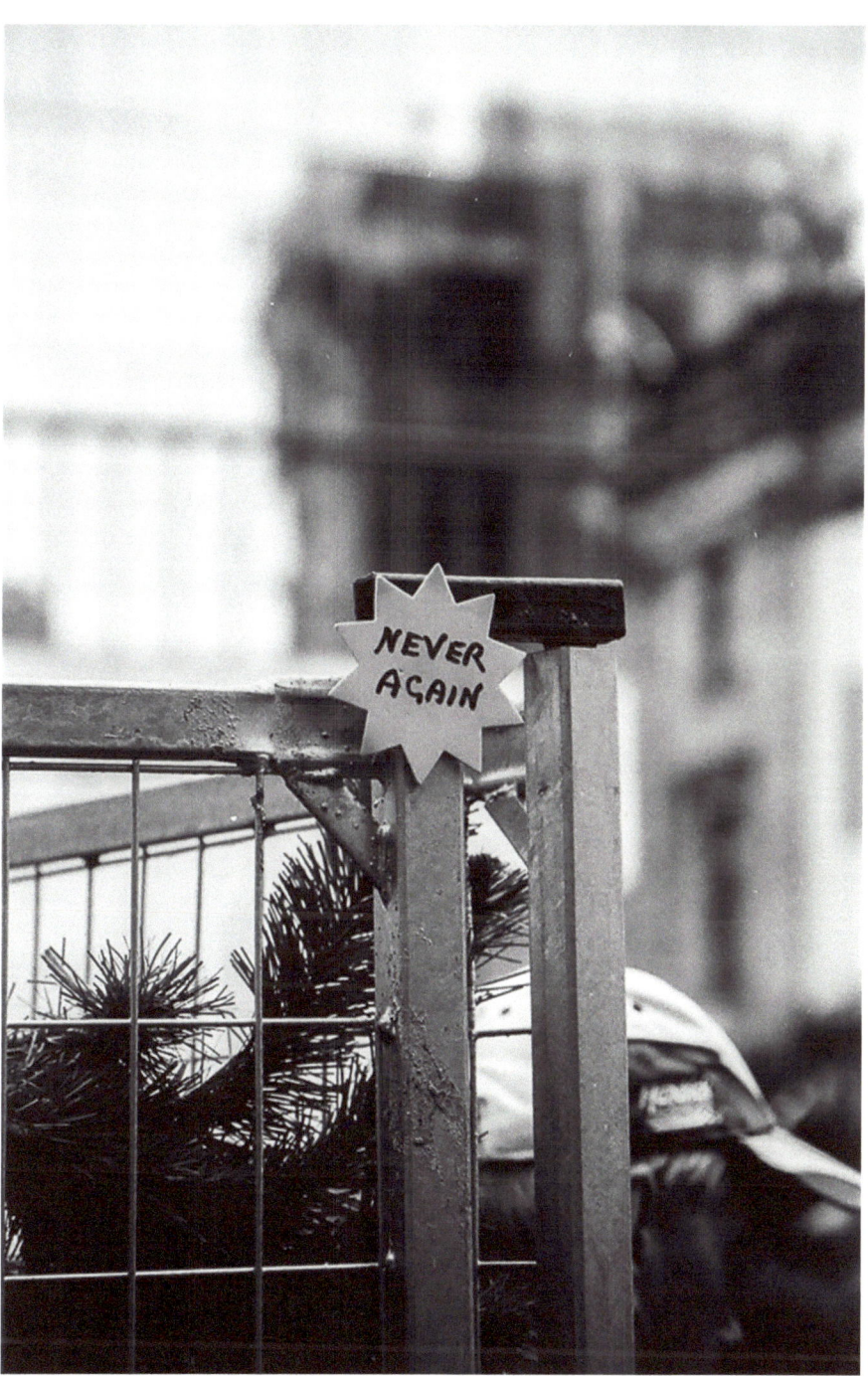

Ilford HP5 Plus

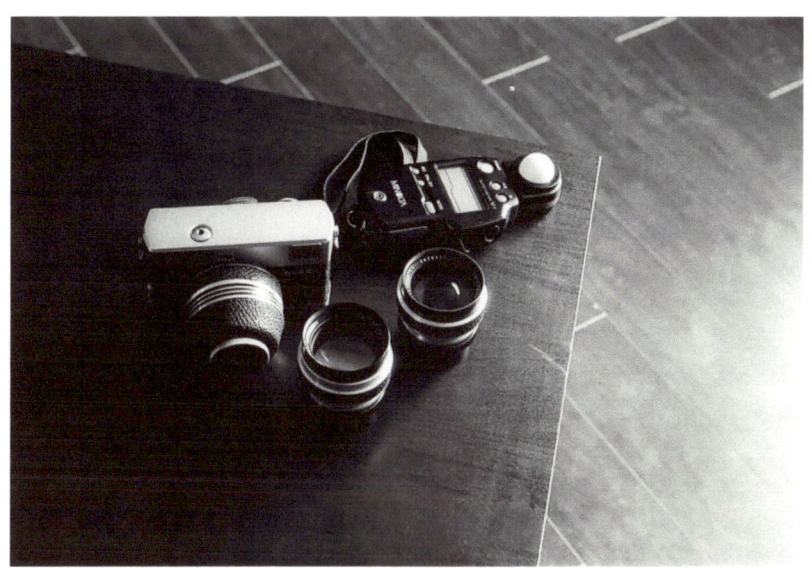

All of the images in this zine were shot by Jason Kilroe with his
Carl Zeiss Jena Werra 3 using 35mm film.

Lenses: Carl Zeiss Jena Tessar 50mm f/2.8
       Carl Zeiss Jena Flektagon 35mm f/2.8
       Carl Zeiss Jena Cardinar 100mm f/4

Film Stocks: Astrum Foto 100
            Kodak Ektrachrome E100
            Iford HP5 Plus

Light Meter: Minolta Auto Meter VF

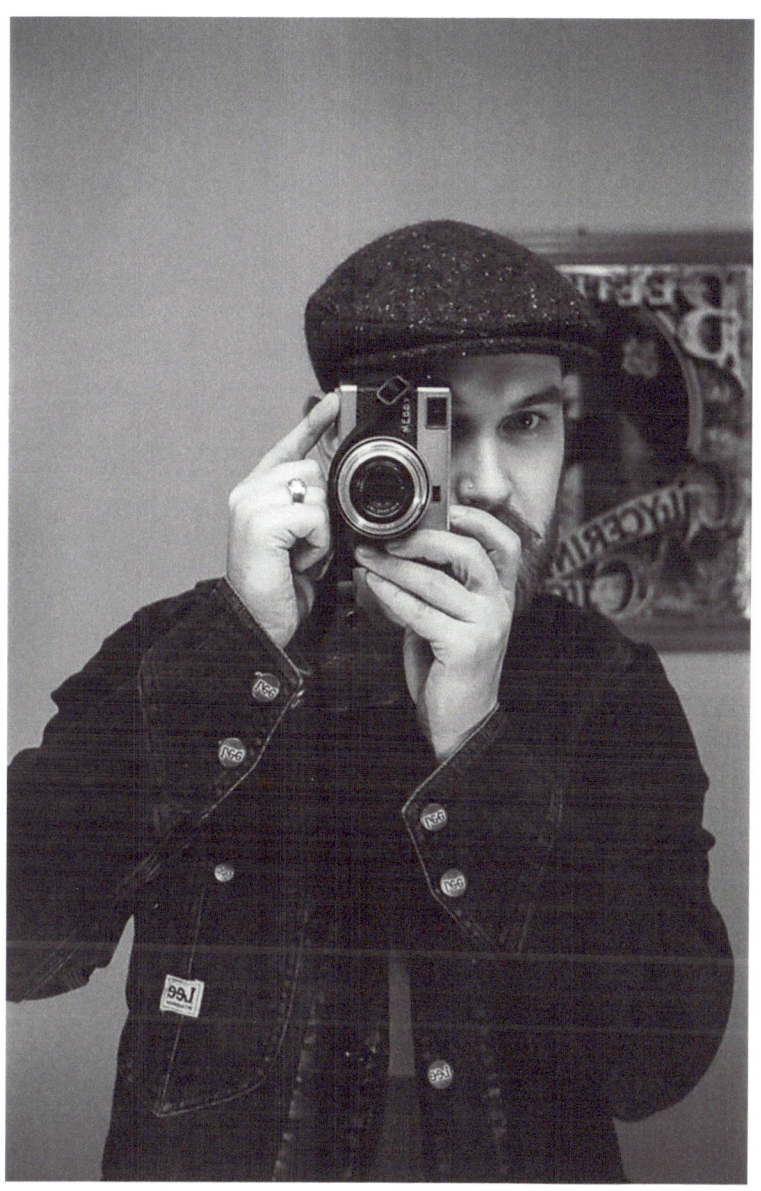

-Jason Kilroe Self Portrait Ilford HP5 Plus

www.ingramcontent.com/pod-product-compliance
Lightning Source LLC
Chambersburg PA
CBHW041944240526
45473CB00033B/505